Painting with Children

When we paint with colours we should paint in such a way that we are conscious that we are calling forth life from what is dead.

Rudolf Steiner [1]

Brunhild Müller

Painting with Children

Floris Books

Translated by Donald Maclean

Photographs of Pictures 7–9, 11–16, 35, 62 by
Dieter Wolk, Winterbach, all others by
Wolpert & Strehle, Fotodesign, Stuttgart
Illustrations by Angelika Wolk-Gerche

First published in German in 1986 under the title
Malen mit Wasserfarben by Verlag Freies
Geistesleben
First published in English in 1987 by Floris Books
Fifth edition 2008
Second printing 2010

British Library CIP Data available

ISBN 978-086315-366-2

Printed in China

Contents

Children and colour

We see the sky in ever-changing colour: in shining blue, almost black in the night, with grey and white clouds, merging into a mysterious violet, flaming up in red, shining in yellow and orange, and in a delicate green within the rainbow. When we gaze around us, colour is everywhere: white snow, grey stone, the blue-green sea, red apples, green meadows, yellow-gold cornfields, violets and brown cows.

From childhood we are immersed in the ever-changing colours of our surroundings. These colours affect our attitude to life, and play into our moods, and are expressed in the colour of our clothes. We delight in wearing our chosen colours.

Children love colours. Babies reach out for coloured objects which attract them. Soon they remember them and remember too the colour sensation that belongs to each colour. Children unite with the colours that flow towards them from their surroundings, even to the extent of feeling inwardly coloured. Children's feelings too are affected strongly by colours. One colour may produce in a child a feeling of well-being, while in another a feeling of discomfort. Because children are so much more receptive than adults their experience of colour is all the more intense.

In their earliest years children's sense perceptions are still fresh. Everything they perceive is imprinted right into their bodies. Thus it cannot be good for a baby to be exposed too soon to harsh daylight, or to have to look into the dead light of an electric lamp. The little baby first perceives light and colour as differentiated shades of brightness. Only when light and colour work upon the eye does it become a perfected organ of sight.

In his book, *The Education of the Child*, Rudolf Steiner illustrates the effect of colour on children:

With regard to the environment, 'nervous' children, that is, excitable children, should be treated differently from those who are quiet and lethargic. Everything comes into consideration, from the colour of the room and the various objects ... around the child, to the colour of the clothes they wear ...

Excitable children should be surrounded by and dressed in red and reddish-yellow colours, while lethargic children should be surrounded by blue or bluish-green shades of colour. The important thing is the complementary colour that is created within the child. In the case of red it is green, and in the case of blue, orange-yellow ...[2]

Right up until they go to school many children call red green and green red, less often blue yellow and yellow blue. Also they may change their favourite colour, like the child whose mother told me that for a long time green had been the child's favourite colour until she was nearly six, when she declared that it was red. This is explained by the fact that children at first experience the complementary colour more strongly than the external colour, and only in the course of time come to experience it as adults do.

The moral effect of colour

In our ordinary life we do not think of colours as independent entities: we are accustomed to regard colours as attributes of things. To the inward vision of the soul, however, the essential nature of each colour can be revealed. Goethe named this the 'sensory-moral effect of colour' or, as Eastlake translates, the 'effect of colour with reference to moral associations.' The following extracts from *Goethe's Theory of Colours* can help us come to a living understanding of colour:

The colours on the plus *side are yellow, red-yellow (orange), yellow-red (minium, cinnabar). The feelings they excite are quick, lively, aspiring.*

Yellow
This is the colour nearest to light. It appears with the slightest mitigation of light, whether through semi-transparent materials or faint reflection from white surfaces. In prismatic experiments it extends alone and widely in the light space, and while the two poles remain separated from each other, and before it mixes with blue to produce green it is seen in its utmost purity and beauty ...

This impression of warmth may be strikingly experienced by looking at a landscape through a yellow glass, particularly on a grey winter's day. The eye is gladdened, the heart expanded and cheered, a glow seems at once to envelop us.

If, however, this colour in its pure and bright state is agreeable and gladdening, and in its utmost power is serene and noble, it is, on the other hand, extremely liable to contamination, and produces a very disagreeable effect if it is sullied, or in some degree tends to the minus side. Thus the colour of sulphur, which inclines to greens has a something unpleasant about it ...

Reddish Yellow

As no colour can be considered stationary, so we can very easily augment yellow into reddishness by condensing or darkening it. The colour increases in energy, and appears, as in red-yellow, more powerful and splendid ...

Yellowy Red

... The active side is here at its highest energy, and we should not be surprised at that impetuous, robust, uneducated people, should especially like this colour ... when children, left to themselves, begin to use tints, they never spare vermillion ...

The colours on the minus side are blue, red-blue, and blue-red. They produce a restless, susceptible, anxious impression.

Blue

As yellow is always accompanied by light, so it may be said that blue brings darkness with it ...

As the upper sky and distant mountains appear blue, so a blue surface seems to retire from us ...

Blue gives an impression of cold, and this, again, reminds us of shade ...

Rooms which are hung with pure blue, appear in some degree larger, but at the same time empty and cold ...

Reddish Blue

... Blue deepens very mildly into red, and thus acquires a somewhat active character, although it is on the passive side. Its exciting power is, however, of a very different kind from that of the red-yellow. It may be said even to disturb rather than enliven ...

In a very attenuated state, this colour is known to us under the name of lilac; but even then it is something lively without gladness.

Bluey Red

This unquiet feeling increases as the hue progresses, and it may be safely assumed that a carpet of a perfectly pure deep blue-red

9

would be intolerable. Whether it is used for dress, ribbons, or other ornaments, therefore it is employed in a very attenuated and light state, and thus displays its character as above defined, in a peculiarly attractive manner ...

Red

... The effect of this colour is as peculiar as its nature. It conveys an impression of gravity and dignity, and at the same time of grace and attractiveness — the former in its dark deep state, the latter in its light attenuated tint; and thus the dignity of age and the amiableness of youth may adorn itself with degrees of the same hue ...

A red glass displays a bright landscape in so dreadful a hue as to inspire sentiments of awe ...

Green

If yellow and blue, which we consider to be the most fundamental and simple colours, are united as they first appear in the first state of their action, the result is the colour which we call green.

This colour is easy on the eye. If the two elementary colours are mixed in perfect equality so that neither predominates, the eye and the mind repose on the result of this mixture as upon a basic colour.[3]

But why is experiencing the colours in this way so important for the human being and especially for the growing child? For younger children the outer and inner worlds are barely separate. Not only do children perceive the colour but at the same time they sense its quality, they feel in themselves its intrinsic nature, and they are conscious of the non-material essential being of such colour. This consciousness is lost as the child grows older, and by the time children go to school they experience colours as attributes of objects (the blue ball, the red roof and so on). And so the ability to feel the different qualities and effects of colours atrophies, and the eye of the soul cannot develop further. Often young children know themselves that red and yellow are warm colours, and green and blue cold, but as they grow older they no longer fully experience this, and so this distinction can easily become abstract and dead knowledge.

Rudolf Steiner therefore advises teachers to let children live and work in the world of colour as soon as possible, immersing themselves in that element of feeling to which Goethe refers in his theory of colour.

Goethe draws our attention to the feelings which the colours arouse in us. He points out the challenging nature of red, and his teaching is as much concerned with what the soul feels when it beholds red, as with what the eye sees. Likewise he mentions the stillness and contemplativeness which the soul feels in the presence of blue. We can present the colours to children in such a way that they will spontaneously experience the shades of feeling engendered by the colours, and will naturally feel the colours' inner life.[4]

Geothe's theory of colour shows 'the relationship of colour to feeling which in turn gives rise to impulses of will.'[5]

Blind people also experience the moral effect of colour. Helen Keller wrote: 'People who can see are wrong when they think that blind people are excluded from all the beauty of colour.'[6] And the blind authoress Ursula Burkhard describes how she was able to form differentiated concepts of colour, particularly with regard to fairy tales, and how she learned to experience inwardly the essence of the colours:

Simple folk-tales said more to me about colours ... When Snow-White's wicked stepmother turned yellow with envy it must have been a poisonous yellow, different from the good nourishing yellow of ears of corn. And in how many moods does the colour red live in 'Snow-White and Rose-Red'! There is the delicate red of the blossom on the rose-bush and the living red of the berries in the wood. Wicked red blazes out of the face of the angry dwarf. The red sky of the morning shines with promise over the precipice where all night long the guardian angel watched over the children who had tarried in the woods. In the redemptory red of the evening the king's son is released from his bear shape, and now we can see him living as a king entirely in red, and wearing, instead of the black rough fur, the mantle of purple-red, the red that is august and regal. [7]

Children also experience colours in fairy tales and thereby form deep and intimate associations with colours.

Children painting with watercolours

The best way to introduce children to colour is to let them paint with colours dissolved in water, because the colour in a liquid form best reveals its nature. Even two- and three-year-old children can manage with a brush and paint. They seize the brush quite spontaneously, dip it in the pot, and paint so that sooner or later the colour spreads out over the whole white sheet of paper (Picture 1). They readily paint with only one colour until the pot is emptied, and then if they take another colour, this will be painted without hesitation over the first. It is the activity of painting and the experience of creating that is all-important here. Nevertheless, the effect of the colour is being unconciously produced in his body. They like painting with water-colours and become happily engrossed.

When children reach the age of three or four they become more aware of the individual colours. Then they begin to put one colour tentatively beside another on the paper, dipping the brush carefully into the pot, and become absorbed in what is happening to the colours on the paper. This process is shown

1.
One colour is happily painted over another by a three-year-old.

2.
First yellow was painted. 'Oh, an angel!'
Then blue was added. 'He's glad.'

3.
Then came red, then blue again, until ...

4.
... the paintbrush was dipped once more into the yellow pot ...

5.
and the picture was finished.

step-by-step in Pictures 2-5.

Love of colour also stimulates four- and five-year-olds to paint with watercolours. Their painting is determined by the individual colours in their various nuances: by what each colour does, and by how it relates to other colours in the process of painting. These children are stimulated by the colours and by everything that is happening on the paper and in the paint pot. Children's delight and enthusiasm are kindled and they often feel a great need for all the other children, brothers and sisters, father and mother to share in their colour experience. Children will make lively comments about their painting and about what is happening with the colours. You can hear comments such as 'My Red is fighting the Blue, he's much stronger, he's pushed the Blue out of the way.' (The blue was so covered by the red that only a little blue strip was visible).

One boy, when he saw the red surrounded by the blue (Picture 6), said: 'My Red is having a rest, he's lying down in the blue bed.'

Another child exclaimed with satisfaction after painting the blue over with red: 'Now the Red has swallowed up the Blue.'

A four-and-a-half-year-old girl cried out happily while painting: 'My Orange is so happy it wants to jump everywhere.' (Picture 7).

6. My Red is having a rest, he's lying down in the blue bed. Boy, aged 4¾.

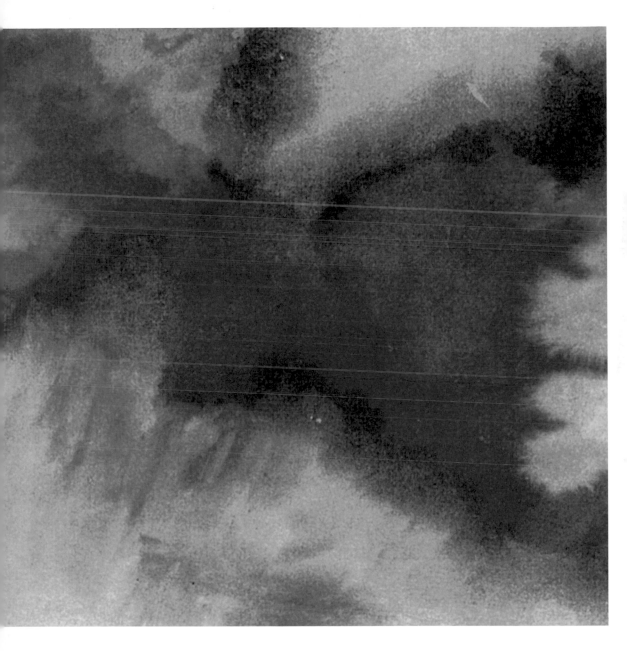

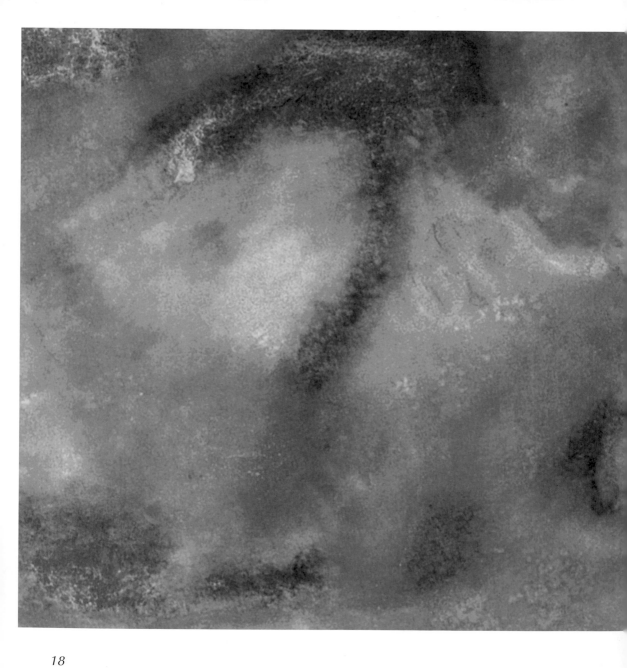

Older children of school age also enjoy colours and painting; they will paint quietly for a while and observe what is taking place on the paper, how one colour meets another, contains it or joins with it, how new colours arise, and what shapes emerge. With their imagination they see all sorts of things in their painting. In Picture 8 one child saw a 'duck,' in Picture 9 a 'castle in the sky.' Picture 10 shows 'the treasure in the cave.'

We can therefore let the child play around with colours because she is following her own formative forces in settling the colours beside each other. She is happy to set one colour beside another, not 'meaning' anything, but with instinctive purpose. Pictures 11 and 12 are examples of this.

When children paint with watercolours we can see, with the first strokes of the brush, two fundamentally different ways of painting. Some children begin by making one patch of colour; then they put further patches of the same or a different colour beside or on top of the first, or they spread the second patches all over the paper (see Pictures 13 and 14). Other children paint lines and shapes (which are then filled in), with the brush as if it were a pencil. While the first set of children are naturally united with the painting process, applying the colour easily and flowingly, the others rarely paint out of direct experience of the colours; they paint more analytically, and they

7
'My Orange is so happy it wants to jump everywhere'.
Girl, aged 4½.

8.
Duck. Girl, aged 5¾.

9.
Castle in the sky. Boy aged 5¼.

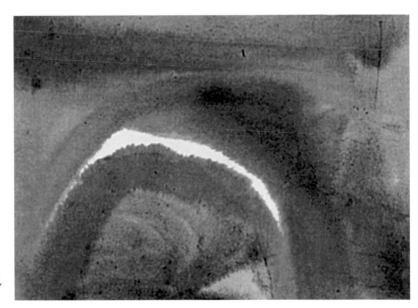

10.
Treasure in the cave. Girl, aged 6.

11
*Red-yellow. Boy,
aged 3½.*

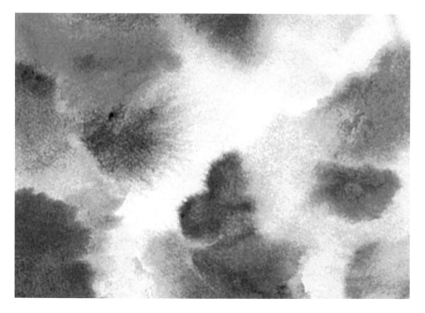

12
*Blue-red-yellow. Girl,
aged 10*

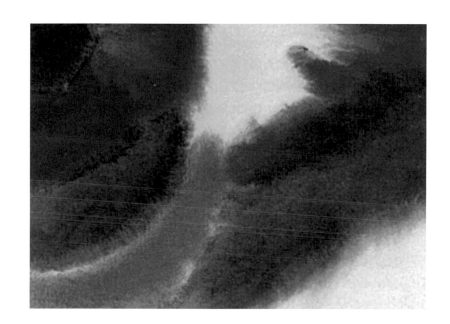

13.
Colour patch.

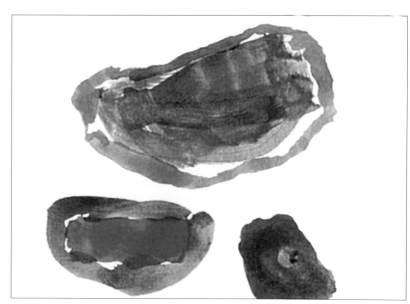

14.
Form outlines.

find it harder to find their way into the play of colours. These children gladly accept any hints by which they can immerse themselves in what is happening with the colours.

Preparing to Paint

Unlike drawing with coloured pencils, chalk, crayons or coloured wax, painting with watercolours requires preparation. This preparation is important for children as it is part of painting, and they should be involved in it.

They will eagerly help to fill the water jars and watch the colour slowly dissolving in the water as they carefully mix it with their brushes. They follow all that is happening as the brushes are washed out in the water and the wonderful colours appear — and already they are involved in the colour process. Often they would like to start painting right away, but first the paper has to be prepared, and here they can also help. We can prepare the paper for younger children in such a way that they can take part in each stage.

1. Mixing the colour

Use water paints from a tube and mix with a fine hair brush (this brush to be used for mixing only). Mix each pot (or glass jar) with enough of one colour to do for all the children. In each case begin with one part paint to two parts water, stir while adding water until the right dilution has been reached (use a damp piece of paper to test.) For yellow you will need more paint than for red. Blue works fine in the proportion of one to two.

2. Distribution

Distribute the mixed colours into little dishes, bowls, saucers, lids, or best of all in little glass jars or pots out of which the colours will shine beautifully. Each child should get one pot of each colour. Two children can share a pot if they already know how to keep their colours clean.

3. Water jars

Fill jam jars three-quarters full of water for cleaning brushes. Each child should have at least one glass, as the water gets dirty very quickly.

4. Preparing the paper

Either dip the paper in a large dish, photo-tray or basin of water so that it absorbs the water evenly, or lay the paper on to the painting board or table and wipe evenly with a wet sponge from side to side, or from top to bottom, or from the centre outwards — but not in a circle, and do not rub or the paper will become roughened. Turn the paper over and repeat the process on the other side. Finally soak up the superfluous water with the sponge and carefully smooth out the bubbles and kinks; this is very important. The size of the paper will depend on what you intend to paint, and should be limited to what the child can manage, but should be at least A4. The paper can be laid flat on the table or on to a board (any paint which gets on to the table at the edge of the picture can be wiped with a damp cloth).

5. Brush and cloth

Only when all this has been done should the child get a brush and cloth (to wipe the brush and to squeeze out superfluous water or paint).

Finally here are some tips about equipment. Use broad flat hair brushes (Nos. 16 or 18) which allow the paint to be applied more delicately. Moreover children can paint layers more easily with them than with bristle brushes. Cheap unglazed drawing paper is more suitable than very smooth paper as the latter has too much clay in it, and does not absorb the water.

Rudolf Steiner gave special indications about the use of watercolours:

We should be specially careful not to let the children use paints straight out of a paintbox. That is wrong even in artistic painting. One should paint out of the dish where the paint has already been mixed with water or other fluid. You must develop an inward intimate relationship to the colour — and so must the child — and you do not have such an intimate relationship to the colour when you paint from the palette, but you develop this when you paint with the colour dissolved in the dish.[8]

Once the preparations are completed a hush of expectancy comes naturally over the children. The brush is then dipped into the jar of water, tested for cleanliness, pressed out with the cloth and dipped into the colour pot. The brush should be wiped two or three times on the edge of the pot before applying the paint to the paper otherwise the application will be too wet.

Painting the colours

Painting with the colours — red, blue, green, yellow, orange, violet, brown, white, grey and black — enables us to get to know their characteristics. To paint with colours means to live with them and in them. Rainer Maria Rilke wrote about Cézanne as follows:

Never has it been so apparent that painting is really an activity that goes on among the colours themselves — that the colours must be left alone to sort themselves out. Painting is the dialogue between the colours themselves: and if anyone interferes by imposing on them his own arrangement, or allows any human consideration, or his own ingenuity, predelection, or mental dexterity to have any say at all in the matter, then the colours will be disturbed and disorientated in their interaction.[9]

Now let us see how these thoughts find a practical application in our painting with children. Already while mixing the colours we give the children indications of what we were going to paint, such as: 'Blue and Red are going to work magic on each other today,' or 'I wonder what Yellow is going to tell Blue,' or if we are going to paint only with blue 'today Blue wants to be alone,' or if we are going to paint with only two red colours — the dark carmine and light vermillion — 'Two red brothers made a bet, who would be the stronger yet.' In this way we can set the direction which will lead the children to the colour. The aim is always to arouse the child's own creativity.

What happens when blue and red work magic on each other will appear on each child's picture, but each child will have produced the result freely in his own way. Even children of pre-school age can get the colours to work magic on each other as the colours themselves demand. They can do this by taking an adult's painting as an example which they do not copy slavishly but can follow freely and individually, and thus become completely engrossed in what they are doing.

Once, we were painting 'Blue, Yellow and Orange are going to play together.' First the children put a little blue, a little yellow and a little orange on to the paper with the brush. One child set all three colours next to each other in the middle of the sheet, while another painted one colour in each corner, and a third spread the colours out in little patches all over the paper. Each child had a different starting point for the game which was about to begin. In Picture 15 you can still see that the boy began painting with bright yellow and powerfully shining orange, leaving spaces free for the blue to be inserted. The picture is mobile and alive; perhaps the colours are playing too?

Colour stories

Sometimes we make up a little colour story while we are preparing the painting, like that told by L. Lionni:

When Yellow found Blue it called out 'Oh there you are! I was looking for you.' Then they laughed and threw themselves into each other's arms, and they were so happy that they turned green as grass.[10]

Guided by this story, as soon as the preparation was completed, the children began to paint with Prussian blue and lemon yellow: along the upper edge they painted a large yellow patch and at the lower edge a smaller blue. Then they brought the yellow down towards the blue, and the blue up towards the yellow. This was repeated several times. Where yellow and blue met, yellow enclosed the blue and permeated it. At first the colours were painted

15.
Blue, Yellow and Orange playing together. Boy, aged 8.

16.
Blue has a birthday. Boy, aged 6.

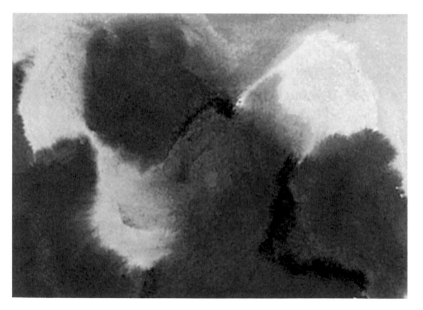

17.
Blue has a birthday. Girl, aged 8½.

gently into each other, then strongly. Later they were painted over each other until in the end, to the deep satisfaction of the children, a strong green was produced.

A similar painting process came about through the colour story of A. Schröder:

A bright glowing Red and a radiantly shining Yellow were friends.

'I would like to be able to shine out as radiantly as you,' said the Red.

'And I would like to glow as brightly as you,' said the Yellow.

Then Yellow gave Red some of the radiant shining and Red gave Yellow some of his bright glowing.[11]

We can find out much about the colours and their relationship with one another if we let red, yellow or blue have a birthday party. The birthday colour is the central colour of the painting process and we start to paint with it. In the following example Blue had a birthday. So Blue was the chief person, and the children painted only blue first on their paper, almost forgetting to leave room for the other colours (which can be seen in Picture 16). But the child stopped painting only blue when guided into a new colour experience with the rhyme:

And now unto the party sped
Two new guests, Yellow and Red.

Now the children brought in plenty of yellow and added the red, as the rhyme went on:

They bring as is on birthdays due
Their special presents to the Blue
They give a cloak, they give a rug
To wrap the Blue up warm and snug.

Then the children painted the red and yellow into the blue. But while they took care not to cover the birthday colour completely their interest was directed much more to the new colours that had been forming: green, orange and violet.

The Blue cried out, 'What's happened here?'
Orange and Green did soon appear,
And Violet too, come stand by me!
And be my friends, you colours three.'

With these words we let the painting come to an end. The children, however, full of what they had seen and done, repeated the rhyme as they were clearing up, and went home happily. Picture 17 is a further example of Blue having a birthday.

Poems too can put a child in the right mood for painting. First we describe what the poem is about, and only at the end of the painting do we recite the poem and let the painting session finish off with it. Examples of suitable poems are given at the end of the book.

Painting through the seasons

A great variety of colour moods can be created by the selection of different colours, and so painting can lead the child to an experience of the seasons and of the festivals of the year. The following suggestions may be adapted to different parts of the world and their climates and festivals.

In winter it is good to use blue — its wealth of tones from light to dark allow a wide variety of form. Real winter pictures can be created on the white paper to the great amazement of children.

In springtime it is a pleasure for the children to paint from delicate lemon yellow to ultramarine blue. Where the blue and yellow mix, a light green is produced, and they (and we) can experience something of the mystery of green. The light and the dark create something new, and in their meeting yellow and blue give up their individual natures.

When the shining colours of tulips and narcissi are visible in the garden, children want to paint with strong colours, golden yellow and vermillion. If they dab red, yellow and blue spots on a green area, they immediately create a happy Easter mood.

In summer we feel like painting with warm red, radiant yellow and shining orange. The red is painted as the brave hero who goes off into battle. Yellow becomes his companion lighting up the whole world.

Once we are into autumn, nature shows herself again in all her diversity of colour. What could be more appropriate than to emulate nature with the paintbrush? Boldly the children set to work, painting with all the colours until they have reproduced the external colourfulness on their paper (pictures 18 and 19).

The autumn mood culminates in Hallowe'en when we can work magic with the colours. How is it done? Let the children make several different red, blue and yellow patches on the paper. Red is the magician who can transform all the blue and yellow patches: the children carefully paint over all the blue patches with red until they become violet and mauve, and all the yellow patches until they become orange. School children especially enjoy doing this, and depending on their temperaments they apply themselves with varying degrees of concentration. We can also paint:

Today Red, the magician, is going around,
Very soon the Yellow he's found
And made him orange without a sound.

18.
*Painting with all the
colours. Girl, aged 7.*

19.
*Autumn tree. Boy,
aged 7.*

Or at Hallowe'en itself:

On Hallowe'en night if only you knew
Quick Red, he played a trick on old Blue.
Old Blue turned red, and Red turned blue,
And no one could tell me who was who.
But all that happened in the best of fun
And now they're both purple all in one.

When outside in November the muted colours, browns and greys, surround us the colours begin to light up within us. The children sense this, and quietly and carefully they wish to paint something specially lovely for father and mother, preferring the blue and violet tones. It is the Advent mood with Christmas at the door:

See in that blue
As dark as night
A star breaks through
Of yellow bright.

The background to stories

If you begin to let children paint in the way we have described you will soon make up your own stories and rhymes. These form an accompaniment to the painting and help the child to enter into a much more intense relationship with the colours. He will begin to talk to the colours and to play with them as if they were human, and while he is painting he is completely at one with them. For the child the activity of painting becomes much more important than the resulting picture. The picture just happens to come into being — often quite a surprise for the child — and the child, full of what is happening, will show his work to everyone. The rhymes and stories are woven into his colour experience and they live on in his memory. This stimulates a mental mobility, which can lead to richer and more versatile concepts and feelings.

Those children who always want to get finished quickly find it difficult to enter into a real experience of colour. But we can help them to go on painting by repeating the rhymes, or with little hints like: 'Your Yellow wants to stream out further,' or 'Yellow wants to give Blue something, I wonder what that will be,' or 'Red hasn't said good morning to Yellow yet.'

Each child requires her own time to get right into the painting activity. One child may be fully in it from the start: another only when the colours appear on the paper and begin to speak to her. This should be kept in mind especially when children are painting in a group, and we should not start cleaning up too abruptly.

Experiencing the colours

Children get to know the characteristics of the colours best when the colours talk and interact with one another during the painting. If the children are painting with only two colours the one colour will behave differently towards the other than if more colours are brought in. Except for two- and three-year-olds, children generally do not find it very satisfying to paint in just one colour, as the single colour soon exhausts what it has to say, and the children are inclined to carry on painting until the paper is quite filled up. Nevertheless we can paint with blue by itself: outlines can be made using light and dark blue: and so 'mountains,' 'waves,' 'cliffs' and 'caves' appear, the latter lighter inside and darker towards the edges. Older children feel the need to paint something with clearer forms, and blue meets this need. Painting in red only can make children quite wild, and a picture painted entirely in red usually looks anything but beautiful. Yellow is the hardest colour to paint by itself because it wants to stream right off the paper. It needs a second colour to help show its shining power.

Violet, orange and green are not simply mixtures of red and blue, red and yellow, blue and yellow respectively, but are self-contained colours within their individual characteristics. Everywhere in nature we come across green in many variations and it speaks to us in many different ways; for example solemnly, even oppressively, in pine trees and holly, and soothing and relaxing in a meadow's green. We feel mauve-violet tones as solemnly festive or sometimes pompous, and orange as cheerful or aggressive.

These three colours, violet, orange and green are independent colours and the children should experience them as such. These colours should therefore be taken straight from the tube and water added. They should not be made by mixing two component colours in one pot. It is quite different when the colours come about during the painting itself. When the children paint red and blue, the violet is produced by the meeting of the two colours; when red unites with yellow they create orange; when blue greets yellow, green results. That is quite different from what children hear or learn when mixing paints: yellow and red make orange, blue and yellow make green, red and blue make violet.

Rudolf Steiner gives an example of how to bring colour experience to school children:

But let us awaken in the child what it means to look at black, red, green, yellow, white. Let us call up in him what it is when we surround a point by a circle. Let us call up the great experience contained in the difference there is when we draw two green circles and in each of them three red circles, then two red and in each of them three green, two yellow with three blue ones in them, then two blue containing three yellow circles. We let the children experience in the colours what the colours as such are saying to the human being, for in the world of colour lives a whole world. But we also let the children experience what the colours have to say to one another, what green says to red, what blue says to yellow, blue to green and red to blue — hence we have the most wonderful relation between the colours.[12]

Moods of nature

Different moods in nature, as for instance in the woods, by water, in the meadows and the contrasts of morning and evening, a thunderstorm, a storm, a hot summer's day, all provide incentives for older children (aged 9 to 13) to paint. But it is important that the motif should emerge from the colours. For morning they can choose the bright, strong, active colours, golden-yellow, vermillion; for evening ultramarine blue, cobalt blue and carmine red. Orange and violet will be produced in the painting process (see Pictures 20 and 21).

In the picture of the thunderstorm (22) black was also used. It was a special experience for the children to see all the different shades of grey coming out when painting with black.

Pictures 23 to 25 were the result of a longer painting lesson. At first the children were painting quite freely — each according to her age, temperament and nature with the colours provided: cobalt blue, ultramarine blue, dark yellow and vermillion. On a second sheet they entered further into these colour harmonies, and then on a third sheet they could each paint their own forms. This resulted in paintings of summer-like flowers.

The flower-meadow picture (27) was painted as a second picture after freely playing with red, yellow and blue (Picture 26).

20.
Morning. Boy, aged 11.

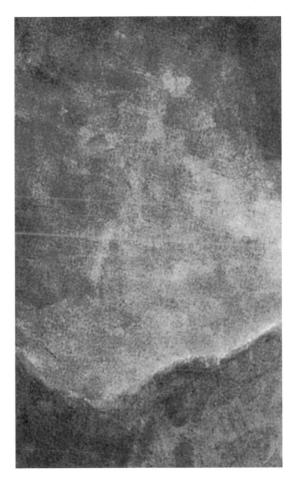

21.
Evening. Boy, aged 11.

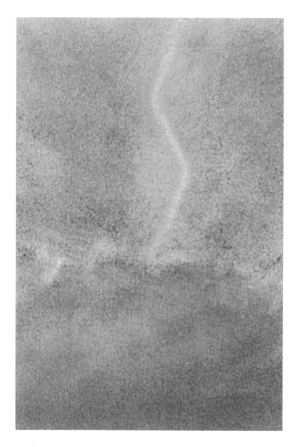

22.
Thunderstorm. Boy, aged 11.

23-25.
Painting process: from colour harmony to picture motif. Girl, aged 11.

Painting what you see

When children paint with watercolours they want to paint what they see around them: trees, houses, streets, cars, aeroplanes, animals, people, the sun, moon and stars. Children do not find it difficult to 'reproduce' all these things with the brush. On the contrary, with the fluid colour on the brush they can let things appear on the paper as they imagine them (Picture 28). In this the children do not feel limited into exactness by definite outlines and exact shapes or by the 'right' colours. This painting is particularly good for children who do not like draw-

26.
Play of colour. Girl,
aged 10.

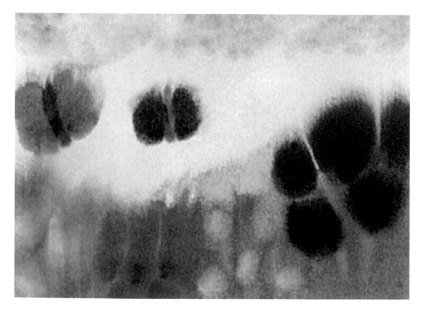

27.
Meadow of flowers. Girl,
aged 10.

28.
Lantern procession. Boy, aged 7½.

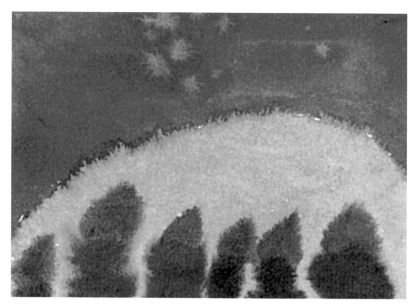

29.
The child first painted the blue patch, then below it the green. Then he put the red spots in the green and partly covered them with blue. The lighter spots in the blue were accidentally caused by water drops, but for the child they became stars shining in the sky above the green mountain with the brownies in the front. Boy, aged 8½.

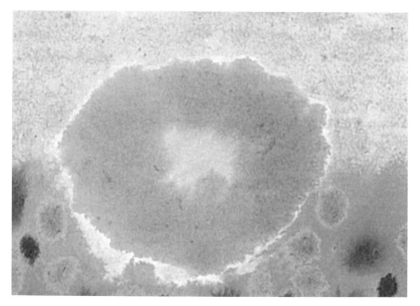

30.
The child began with yellow, putting it in the middle of the picture and surrounding it with a delicate blue. Then green came into contact with it. When she began to dab red, yellow and blue dots in the green she said: 'That's the Easter-sun, and the Easter eggs are lying in the grass.' Girl, aged 8¾.

ing with crayons, felt-tips or coloured chalk. Painting with brushes and watercolour helps these children to express themselves artistically.

Pictures 29 and 30 show how children paint out of the colours themselves. Soon the colours gave the picture a mood and from the moods the child found the motif for her picture.

The transition to the painting of objects should not be determined from outside but should derive from the colours themselves. Gradually blue becomes something that retreats into the distance, red and yellow something coming forward. Thus a sense of colour perspective is developed which can later serve as a basis for geometrically constructed perspectives. Rudolf Steiner even states that it is 'harmful to teach an older child perspective if he has not discovered intense colour perspective beforehand.'[13]

Painting with plant colours

Painting with plant colours gives children further ways to identify themselves with colour in the world. Just as the colours in nature permeate and flow into each other — as in the sky or in the dewdrop — and just as they shine, shimmer and radiate where there is moisture, so we experience them when painting with plant colours.

When the colours are being prepared, children watch in astonishment as the colour substances transform. Then later when they start to paint they are surprised to find that now the colours on the paper are not nearly as strong as they were in the pot, and this does not change when the colours are painted over several times. Even then the colours retain their delicacy and purity. Where one colour is laid over another very delicate colour nuances and gentle transitions into new colour tones arise.

In this way children feel that there is something special about these plant colours and consequently love painting with them. It appears as if the children through the plant colours are touched by the magic of the living elemental world (Pictures 31 and 32).

Preparation for painting with plant colours

is different from preparing watercolours. Pound the colour powder (about a quarter of a teaspoon) and the resin emulsion (3 or 4 drops) in a mortar with a pestle and leave to stand for a few minutes. The grains can also be ground first and the emulsion added. Add water drop by drop (using a clean paintbrush or dropper) and continue mixing until the water, powder and emulsion are evenly distributed. The length of time required is different for each colour. Now dilute the solution further in a jar by slowly adding water from a jug. Take care not to make the solution too watery (especially with red and yellow), because the little specks of pigment cannot be thinned out. The powdery colour in glass tubes is preferable to the ready-mixed colours in bottles or jars because it can be used more economically, it keeps better and the colours are purer. Also the mixing of the materials in the mortar and the preparation of the colours are important experiences for the children, belonging as they do to the whole process of painting with colours.

With plant colours you can paint on any white, unglazed watercolour paper. The paper should only be slightly dampened before painting, otherwise the colour will float on the surface, and once the paper has dried the colour will lie on it in little granules. To suit the delicacy of the colours use brush No. 18. After painting, first clean the brush with a little soap to prevent it clogging and becoming hard, then wash out thoroughly. Any unused colour can be poured back into the mortar where it can dry and be used again with two or three drops of resin emulsion and a very little water.

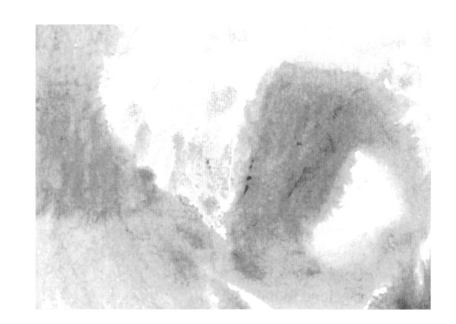

31.
Cave. Boy, aged 5.

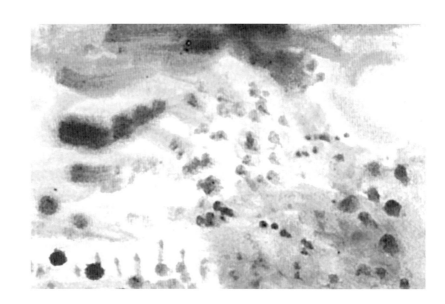

32.
Midsummer mood.
Boy, aged 4¾.

Poems

My Lady Spring

My Lady Spring is dressed in green,
She wears a primrose crown,
And little baby buds and twigs
Are clinging to her gown;
The sun shines if she laughs at all,
But if she weeps the raindrops fall.

(Unknown)

Spring

Now daisies pied, and violets blue,
And lady-smocks all silver white,
And cuckoo-buds of yellow hue
Do paint the meadows with delight.
The cuckoo now on every tree
Sings cuckoo, cuckoo.

Shakespeare

White Sheep

White sheep, white sheep
On a blue hill,
When the wind stops
You all stand still.
You all run away
When the winds blow;
White sheep, white sheep,
Where do you go?

W. H. Davies

Violets

I know, blue modest violets
Gleaming with dew at morn –
I know the place you come from
And the way that you are born!

When God cast holes in heaven –
The holes the stars looks through –
He lets the scraps fall down to earth;
The little scraps are you!

(Unknown)

O Dandelion

'O Dandelion, yellow as gold,
What do you do all day?'

'I just wait here in the tall green grass
Till the children come to play.'

'O Dandelion, yellow as gold,
What do you do all night?'

'I wait and wait till the cool dews fall
And my hair grows long and white.'

'And what do you do when your hair is white
And the children come to play?'

'They take me up in their dimpled hands
And blow my hair away!'

(Unknown)

Red in Autumn

Tipperty-toes, the smallest elf,
Sat on a mushroom by himself,
Playing a little tinkling tune
Under the big round harvest moon;
And this is the song that Tipperty made
To sing to the little tune he played.

'Red are the hips, red are the haws,
Red and gold are the leaves that fall
Red are the poppies in the corn,
Red berries on the rowan tall;
Red is the big round harvest moon,
And red are my new little dancing shoon.'

Elizabeth Gould

Winter Joys

White stars falling gently,
Softly down to earth,
Red fires burning brightly
In the warm and cosy hearth.

White trees changed to elfin-land,
By red sun's dazzling glow,
Little robin redbreasts
Hopping in the snow.

Happy children's voices,
Shouting loud with glee,
Oh! the joys of winter
Are wonderful to me.

Dorothy Gradon

Colour

The world is full of colour!
'Tis autumn once again
And leaves of gold and crimson
Are lying in the lane.

There are brown and yellow acorns
Berries and scarlet haws
Amber gorse and heather
Purple across the moors!

Green apples in the orchard,
Flushed by a glowing sun;
Mellow pears and brambles
Where coloured pheasants run!
Yellow, blue and orange,
Russet, rose and red –
A gaily coloured pageant –
An Autumn flower bed.

Beauty of light and shadow,
Glory of wheat and rye,
Colour of shining water
Under a sunset sky!

Adeline White

Many other examples may be found, as for instance, Wordsworth's 'Daffodils.'

References

1. Rudolf Steiner, *Practical Advice to Teachers* (lecture August 23, 1919) Anthroposophic Press, New York.
2. Rudolf Steiner, *The Education of the Child,* pp.20f. Anthroposophic Press, New York 1996.
3. Johann Wolfgang Goethe, *Farbenlehre.* An English translation was published as *Theory of Colours,* Cambridge, Mass. & London 1970.
4. Rudolf Steiner, *Practical Advice to Teachers* (lecture August 23, 1919) Anthroposophic Press, New York.
5. Rudolf Steiner, *The Foundations of Human Experience* (lecture August 29, 1919) Anthroposophic Press, New York 1996.
6. Helen Keller, *Out of the Dark,* 1913.
7. Ursula Burkhard, *Farbvorstellung blinder Menschen,* Basel 1981.
8. Rudolf Steiner, *Soul Economy and Waldorf Education* (lecture January 3, 1922) Anthroposophic Press, New York.
9. R.M. Rilke, *Briefe über Cezanne,* Frankfurt 1983.
10. L. Lionni, quoted in A. Schröder, *Farbgeschichten,* Stuttgart 1984.
11. A. Schröder, *Farbgeschichten,* Stuttgart 1984.
12. Rudolf Steiner, *The Younger Generation,* p.133f. Anthroposophic Press, New York 1976.
13. Rudolf Steiner, *The Child's Changing Consciousness* (lecture April 19, 1923) Anthroposophic Press, New York.